From Home to Home: Through the Eyes of an Immigrant

Cover Artwork: Maria Liana Moisescu
Cover Writer: Ava Mallory
Illustrations: Pixabay / Pexels / Unsplash /
Witches: five silhouetted figures. Credit: Wellcome Collection
CC BY / 5000 Designs and Motifs from India by Ajit Mookerjee
Editor: Preeti Pavaday

from HOME to HOME

Through the Eyes of an Immigrant

BY

KUMAR CHANDRA

O Lord,

From the illusion of separateness,
Lead me to the real truth of Oneness;
From the pain of ego and selfishness,
Lead me to the joy of Selflessness;
From worldly birth, death and strife,
Lead me to the peace of Immortal Life:

From the unreal, lead me to the Real,
From darkness, lead me to Light,
From death, lead me to Immortality.

Dedication

Submitted at the lotus feet of

The Divine

Sri Sathya Sai Baba

Table of Contents

Introduction By The Author

What's the first thing I remember about England? Probably the lights at the airport lounge. At first sight, not only were there more than enough to light up an entire city, but the halls were absolutely spick-and-span, much more than I had ever imagined. Come to think of it, there were many aspects of Heathrow Airport that exceeded my expectations: the polished floor was not only elaborate but very clean; the air was fresh with a light hint of fragrance, probably being wafted from the duty-free; the baggage retrieval and all the formalities were done in a controlled manner as opposed to the chaos that I had generally been used to. After baggage retrieval, the Immigration Officer asked me nonchalantly: "I see you're joining us from India: what is the reason for your visit?" The emotionally worn-out side of me just wanted to say: "I've got nothing to go back to", but the rational side of me won the inner battle, and I ended up saying: "I'm here for my studies", a mere half-truth for convenience sake.

I came to England in 1958 with my younger sister, when I was a teenager. My mother and my elder sister had already moved to England a year earlier. The above is an account of the first thing I remember after travelling from Calcutta Airport to Heathrow. I remember that day so clearly since that was the biggest journey that I had ever embarked on, literally and emotionally speaking. Believe it or not, we were actually not fond of change! However, when actions are driven out of dire necessity, then it becomes a very different matter.

We moved out of India due to our family being hit by financial difficulties due to the political and socio-economic scene in Bihar (India) at that time. Any governmental change would affect us particularly hard since my father worked directly within the political sector. One such change occurred that triggered off a series of events which resulted in him losing his position. We had to sell off our possessions in order to keep our house, then losing the house and finally relocating to England. The whole ordeal was hard to endure since we essentially ended up with starting from scratch. However, moving to England is a decision I've never regretted since it gave us shelter, job and funding for our education. We began to feel that England was our second home. So, I've always viewed my migration as leaving one home and being welcomed to a new home: "When the Lord closes the door, He always leaves a window open."

Whilst the past is not something that I like to visit all too often, I do believe in finding the hidden lessons from these tough conditions. Personally, I think that we are put into a difficult situation to learn a lesson from it, and then to do the hardest thing of all: be grateful for it. I am grateful to have gone through financial hardship in India since it has not only revised my relationship with money, but it also provided me the chance to start anew, and to raise my own children in a prosperous country: to give them the opportunities that I myself never had. It also gave me the experience to remain calm in the face of adversity, and the confidence to face difficulties that life would throw at me. So, I took it as a challenge to not only find the lesson, but to write it down in a beautiful format: in the form of poetry.

As a teacher of Maths and Science and all things logical, it's quite ironic that I would be more gravitated towards poetry. However, poetry, I felt, was the appropriate medium to express myself, specifically traditional poetry with a set structure. Some may say that it stunts creativity by adding restrictions, but I like to think of it like solving a puzzle i.e. to get it correct rhythmically, following a rhyming scheme whilst not compromising the tone, pace and quality of the actual narrative, and writing to a reasonable standard. In a sense, all of the stars needed to align for this seemingly impossible task, which is probably why it has taken more than 20 years in the making!

"From Home To Home" is a collection of poems that reflects the beauty that I see in the world, and all the lessons that I've drawn from it. Like most art-forms, writing poetry is more of a compulsion that comes from within whenever inspiration strikes, not something that is premeditated or planned neatly: it's a mess, an entanglement of thoughts that I had to carefully iron out into something that resembles a poem, on topics that are close to me. It wasn't until I had finished writing my poems and begun curating them into a book format that I realised that my seemingly random assortment of poems could actually be categorised into the following "themes" which make up this book:

1) **My Romance with England:** I've always loved the inherent beauty that the different landscapes of England has to offer. The archaic architecture of castles speaks to the traditionalist in me, and the culturally diverse and whimsical ethos of London speaks to the eccentric artist in me. England relates to most of the facets of my personality, so much so that it is impossible not to be inspired by it. Hence I've dedicated the first seven poems to England (1. "My England, My Home" to 7. "The Sea Beach").

2) **The Seasons in England:** The weather seems to be a pretty big deal to all of us in England although if we look at it closely, it is probably the best in the world. Such close examination can dress the same place you've seen for years in a different way and reveal new aspects of its character. In a way, this section is an extension of the previous section. The poems 8. "Spring in England" to 13. "Snowfall" make this category.

3) **My India:** Even though I have practically spent more of my life till now in England, my foundations were laid originally in India. In this section, I have chronicled the key memories that have gone on to shape my core outlook on life. I have also touched upon the concept of "Seasons" again, to contrast its sight in India with that in England. The poems 14. "A Tropical Sunset at Sea" to 17. "The Burst of The Monsoon" reflect this.

4) **Childhood Days:** As a school-teacher, education is paramount to me. I have seen many of my students go through the arduous journey of adolescence with the added complexity of earning a stable education at the same time. However, they still managed to turn out to be strong, multi-dimensional individuals who have extended the core values they learnt from their education into their lives, with a potential and a promise to change the world for the better. Poems 18. "Childhood Days" to 22. "True Education" are offered to these students.

5) **War:** Whilst personally I have not witnessed any war, I have had first-hand accounts from friends who have. They were mainly involved in the Indo-Sino war that broke out in the 1960s. Their account of what transpired there moved me, since it takes a certain type of mental fortitude

and loyalty for one's country to be involved in it. These values are the likes of which I hold in great esteem and what I aspire to have. Poems 23. "A Soldier's Dream Maiden" to 25. "A Soldier's Dilemma" are in honour of these war heroes.

6) **Lessons from Animals:** I have always found animals to be very innocent in nature and there is always a lot we can learn from them. Poems 26. "My Pet" to 36. "The Donkey Ride" are devoted to them.

7) **Stories:** This forms a large portion of the book as it is the collection of lessons that I have been taught by one of the greatest teachers: Time. The lessons are mostly framed in a story format so that they can easily resonate with readers. Originally, many of them happen to be famous, ancient fables for kids; however, the core message remains relevant and important to both children and adults alike, even to this day. Poems 37. "The Loyal Scarecrow" to 45. "Compassion" shape this section.

8) **Miscellaneous:** This section is part-philosophical and part-social. These poems happen to be topics that I have always wanted to give my opinion on, be it in a satirical sense or in earnest. However, they do not fall into any of

the categories mentioned above (poems 46. "Music" to 54. "Poetry").

As mentioned earlier, hardly any planning was done in the beginning, as I was simply eager to write something; the only aspect that was deliberate was the number of poems. I have written exactly 108 poems since this is an auspicious number in Hinduism. This book contains the first 54 poems, and the remaining will be in the second book. Whilst this book concentrates on how one can experience this world outwardly and practically, the second book focuses on experiencing the same world inwardly and spiritually.

Finally, I must mention how deeply indebted I am to my wife and family, and to my friends, relatives and well-wishers – all of whom have made valuable contributions to all aspects of my writing. It is partly under some pressure from them that I am releasing some of my writing in the form of an anthology of 108 poems, spread over two books.

My Romance with England

1

My England, My Home

England is my heart's garden,
Making happiness grow and widen;
Wherein the prettiest blooms grow
And a soothing wind does blow–
Which have the charm and sweetest scent
To cure the mind of any torment.

My Garden's blooms are its people,
Working for a just principle:
Valuing fairness, and full justice
In every design and practice;
Such are the folks who make the story
Of my land of hope and glory.

My Garden has a charming clime,
Four clear seasons minding time:
Spring's song-birds, and blossoms fair,
Summer's warm, romantic air,
Autumn's changing, leafy glow,
And winter's white and flaky snow.

The land is always emerald green,
The seas around have sapphire sheen;
Its rolling plains are a poet's gem,
And coastal sands are pearls in a hem;
Its rivers make the finest scenes:
The river Wye and its woodland greens.

And if I venture overseas,
My mind is never set at ease
To think I'm far, from my Garden,
Making my own resolve harden:
Never to leave my Garden and roam,
Never to journey away from home.

I couldn't exchange my dear England
For any prize or any fund,
As this would take my only gem
And put my mind in full mayhem.
My England, I'm forever thine,
Be it rain, or be it shine.

2

My London

My London shows its glory
From the monuments on the Thames,
Where the buildings tell the story
In a host of cultural gems:

The Parliament building in stone,
The Tower Bridge in iron cast,
And Saint Paul's in no less tone
Remind us of the glorious past.

London has a temperate clime:
Neither hot, nor too cold;
Four clear seasons blend the time
Into a charming, soothing mould.

The city has a natural beauty,
For its paths were never planned;
They arose from need and duty,
Not designed by office hand.

London's suburbs are efficient,
Self-contained in themselves,
Where things of need are sufficient
And food enough for kitchen shelves.

The city excels in flowers–
Regent's Park with cosy bowers:
Roses casting magical powers
On the mind in blissful showers.

Its diners serve the best gravy,
Museums top the world of art;
Its Jewels are the world's envy
And theatres are a class apart.

Being so diverse and mighty–
A whole world within a city–
London puts boredom to the knife:
Bored of London, is bored of life!

But my London's greatest asset
Lies in sheltering every culture;
And in this way, it has met
All demands, of Scripture:

Treating all in equal light
Regardless of their race or creed,
It ascends in moral height–
A beacon for the world to heed.

3

London By Night

As I strolled from the Strand
On to Waterloo Bridge at night,
I saw a view most truly grand–
A city decked in colour and light.

Lights have always gripped my mind:
Fireworks, Christmas, floating lanterns;
But this show, was one of a kind,
Making up a million patterns.

To my left, the lights just rolled
From Saint Paul's to the Wharf–
Buildings lit up, both new and old–
The Shard labelling them a dwarf.

To my right, was Festival Hall
Flashing lights and colours in bold,
The London Eye was pink and tall,
The Big Ben capped in green and gold.

And beneath me, I could see
Lights from boats, in a dancing drill,
The Thames reflecting this spree
Holding the mind, and vision still.

The moon above, was shining bright
And stars around, were joining in,
To outshine London by night
Despite the odds against their win.

So, from my left and from my right,
From below, and from the sky,
I was soaked in dazzling light–
Whose spell, I couldn't deny.

Surprise and joy at the sight
Made me think of all things nice:
Could this be an Arabian Night
Or Fairyland in Paradise?

4

London's Southbank

London's Southbank has the songs
For which my heart forever longs;
It has the rhythms to allay
A sullen mind and make it sway:
The concerts held within its walls
Invoke the very highest calls–
Be it classical, jazz or band
Or just a thrilling, circus hand.

I adore the ethos there:
The feel of a joyous fair,
The grounds around, and everywhere,
Breathing the light, refreshing air
Among the people, out to share
Joy and mirth, without a care–
Relaxed, with a cheerful flair:
Some in groups, and some in pair.

It has galleries, with exhibits,
Which can thrill viewers to bits;
Skateboarding, and second-hand books:
The haunt of youths, in scruffy looks;
Painted men, posing as rock,
Then moving, to give a shock;
And magical folks, with sleights of hand,
Places where I love to stand.

An open-bus tour leaves from here
And guided boat-rides from the pier,
The flashing tubes of the Arcade
Enclose a funfair-type parade,
The big wheel of the London Eye
Has lofty views across the sky;
Then there is the famed Aquarium:
Europe's largest fish symposium.

The Southbank faces Thames stream:
A show of boats, like in a dream;
The homes beyond, and the Big Ben,
Seem like drawings from a pen;
A footbridge also leads from here,
Completing an image fair and dear–
Making a real picture-card,
Prompting the writings of a bard.

The evening sees the sun invite
One and all to the Southbank site:
To see it setting and ignite
The whole sky with coloured light.
Then, bridges too adorn a sight,
Blue and gold, ruby and white,
The facing buildings in floodlight,
The Thames making them doubly bright.

The lighted boats bring waves that fight
To catch a sparkle with their might;
Blinking stars join in at night
From their own angelic height;
The air is cool and feeling right
Holding the breath simply tight;
The London Eye has no respite
And yet it seems to beam delight.

As night proceeds, the tone changes:
Romance and courtship then ranges;
The brisk activity of the noon
Settles to the coolness of the moon:
Whispering pairs take up their seat
In candle-light to gaze and meet;
The air is ripe for love and date,
Ending the lovers' daylong wait.

But, I take leave at the end of day,
And does it matter what they say?
I go there to roam and wander,
Bring home bliss, to cherish and ponder.
The Southbank has unique effect,
From which the mind cannot defect:
Uplifting, haunting, stress-relieving–
The one experience worth believing!

5

A Visit to Windsor Castle

London to Windsor Riverside:
A most delightful train ride,
With scenes across the window panes
Of country greens and leafy lanes.

At Windsor, the air is light,
Blooms abound, people polite:
Lively tourists fill the place,
Soaking history at their pace.

The first sight, that's on display,
Is Windsor Bridge, of ancient day,
Across a shimmering, shining sheet,
Reflecting the sun's dancing feet.

The famous swans are just below,
Snow-white, in a picture show,
Near to where the boats leave
For the scenic drive they weave:

The boats glide through flowered reed,
Ducks of different colour and creed
And anglers flaunting fishing feat–
The view from Thames, a real treat!

A charming bus-ride shows landmarks,
The Long Mile and the famous parks–
Then across to Datchet village,
Eaton and its wide spillage.

And there is a bright funfair
Scattering mirth everywhere;
A giant wheel is also there,
Lending views across the air.

Then there are antiques to shop
And places where diners could drop,
With ancient houses all around
Displaying Windsor's royal background.

The Castle has imposing form,
An awesome build by any norm,
Looking down from higher ground,
Dwarfing houses all around.

The entrance hall has weapons of old,
Linking history, set in bold:
Swords in floral design,
Guns on walls, looking benign.

The interior is a piece of art–
Crafts surrounding every part:
Chandeliers, china, paintings of old,
Furniture, tapestry, mirrors in gold.

However, what stands out most
Is *silence*, which the walls do host:
How I wish the walls could speak
And fill the gap historians seek:

On royal romance, and heartbreak,
On the shape, envy could take,
On the plots, that kings do make,
And the fears, which make them shake.

On me, the trip has left a spell,
Calling the mind to turn and dwell
On the harmony of the place–
Nature and pomp in full embrace:

The natural beauty that surrounds,
Takes in the Castle and its bounds,
Making Windsor quite unique–
A perfect gem which poets seek!

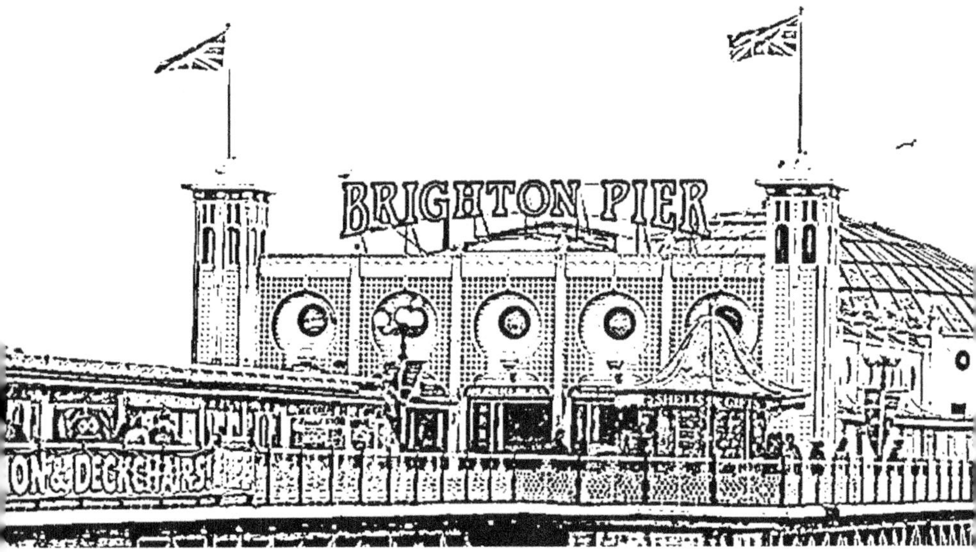
BRIGHTON PIER
ON & DECKCHAIRS!

6

A Trip to Brighton

Victoria to Brighton by train,
Gives the view of a mighty plain
Of the most populous kind,
Nurturing homes of every find.

We arrive at Brighton Station,
Perhaps unique in the nation:
With a ceiling made of curved arches
And old-time lamps on these branches.

We first explore Brighton Pavilion–
Finest home in my opinion,
With Indian art on the outside
And Chinese décor carved inside:

Built by an opulent prince
Who loved to show and convince
His royal guests from everywhere
That he had the finest flair:

The Dining room has a pompous ceiling,
The Music room is art-revealing,
The Drawing rooms are treasure-dives,
The Library filled with great archives.

Then on to the Sea-life Centre,
Which impresses as we enter:
A huge Aquarium, in limited quarters,
With a glass tunnel through its waters.

This glass walkway is unique,
A wonderful display technique,
Winding through a man-made sea
With sharks as close as they can be!

A guided bus-tour waits outside,
Tempting tourists to take a ride;
The open-top gives clear views
Of the resort's changing hues.

The tour carves through narrow lanes,
Boutiques and flowered terrains,
Besides scanning the very sea-front,
Inspecting each bather's stunt.

It drives past impressive hotels,
Private homes and garden motels,
The full sea on the other side,
Sparkling in the sun with pride.

It passes a road with culinary graces,
Having a hundred eating places!
And then goes through another road
With every house a painted abode!

It reaches the Marina Complex
By a maze of roads, that does perplex;
This has great shopping commitment,
And a full dining fulfilment.

The tour ends at the pier,
The vast sea being so near,
The pier packed with so much fun:
Amusements, rides, cream and bun!

Yet, at the pier, what strikes most
Is the view of the crescent coast–
From the balcony of the pier,
The full panorama being so clear:

People lying on the beach,
Hotels painted in cream and peach,
The dancing waves at such close reach,
The sea-gulls' own distinctive screech:

Children playing on the sand
With parents sunning close at hand;
Folks on chairs, relishing the breeze,
Soaking the sun, and feeling at ease.

The evening sees a mist gathering,
Daylight fading, mood faltering;
But then the promenade soon brightens–
And with this, the spirit heightens:

Coloured bulbs pave the way
And floodlit hotels line the bay–
Courting couples stroll in fashion,
Lifting Brighton to a new dimension!

7

The Sea Beach

Here I stand
With pebble in hand,
On golden sand
With a view so grand:

Couples are sunning,
Children running
Showing their cunning
At castles stunning.

The pier is humming,
Vendors drumming,
Stalls jamming,
Casinos cramming.

There are rides,
The usual slides,
Water glides,
Trains besides.

A merry festivity,
Fair creativity–
Apt connectivity
To joyous activity:

For we are joyful,
Essentially cheerful,
Forever hopeful,
Seeking the blissful!

Seasons in England

8

Spring in England

Spring arrives to give out joy
To every creature bold or coy,
When Nature sings in open voice:
"Spring is here, and so rejoice."

Winter's mist is almost gone
And grass is greener in the lawn;
It *is* a cheering, warming sight,
And the cold– it does not bite!

Nature is princely reborn,
Lambs fun-play, and trees adorn
A gentle green of lightest hue,
Inspiring all, for journeys new.

Barest trees, blossom to colour,
Surprising all, in their valour–
Filling every part of tree
With countless flowers set in glee:

The cherry and the magnolia,
Azaleas and the camellia–
Are among those, that re-light
To make Spring special and bright.

The young birds sing from morn to eve
And bees are not prepared to leave;
The cubs of fox just gaze at tree
In a daze what they could be!

Notes ring out from tuneful thrush,
Squirrels take on the tree-top rush–
And all these bounties leave imprint
Of great solace and joyful hint:

For when I am in a mood quite dark,
My mind recalls the singing lark
And all the song-birds of Spring,
Which take my heart upon their wing.

9

A Woodland Sunrise in Spring in England

The first colours of dawn are out,
A new day is about to sprout;
The stars decide it's time to go,
Giving way to a changing glow;
A streak of pink sits high on cloud,
Nestlings become vocal and loud;
The night's chorus hides in heathers:
The woodland sings of songs from feathers.

The sky then turns a golden mellow,
Painting the earth in lightest yellow;
The hiding sun struggles to tear
Through the mist of morning air;
Strings of ducks, fly past on high,
In a line, across the sky;
The woodland rings of flutter and hum,
Activity reigns, where things seemed numb.

The trees reveal a lightest green
With new-born leaves in brightest sheen;
And fragrant bluebells come to light
With tiny daisies dressed in white;
Dandelions raise their head
As yellow stars on a purple bed;
And tangled creepers make it clear:
Their creamy flowers are most dear.

The Sun breaks out behind the trees!
And rays fan out in scented breeze;
The beams of gold come through a mist
And give the place a sudden twist:
The dew on trees and leafy heaps
Become diamonds, as magic sweeps;
Sparkling gems light up the wood,
Defying belief as nothing could.

The woodland freshness of Spring,
The songbirds in full swing,
New-born life in celebration,
The air of warmth and jubilation,
Coupled with the charm all around–
Leave the senses hushed and spellbound;
A poet placed in such a land
Is firmly cast in fairyland.

Nature is ever so proud to tell–
None can quell the woodland spell:
"My woodland-sunrise in Spring
Will put you on a mighty sling
And fling you into realms unseen
Where only poetry has been;
And then, it *will* steal your sleep,
Making you wait, for dawn to creep."

10

Summer in England

Summer comes to give us cheer,
When days are long, no chill to fear;
Then it's time for lakeside walks
And visiting woods, where Nature talks.

The fields adorn lively attire,
And buttercups are a golden fire;
Daisies brighten weedy herbs
And roses deck the garden kerbs.

Butterflies spread their wings,
Humming bees go round in rings;
Chirping crickets liven the night,
Croaking frogs add ballads bright.

On country lanes, the branches meet,
With birds on high in a dancing feat;
The thrush's call, the blackbird's cry
Spread romance across the sky:

In sheltered nooks, young lovers meet
And pairing doves each other greet
While Nature has its daintiest show
To fill the lovers' heart with glow.

Anglers pass the day with hooks
Along the silvery bubbling brooks,
And dreaming cattle often miss
Returning home from Summer's bliss!

To me all these and many more
Give the features I adore,
But my pen is lost for flair
In describing Summer's air:

It sheds a charm to drift around
And fly and float above the ground–
To mount a cloud, up in the sky,
And watch at ease the world go by!

11

Autumn in England

It is autumn's colourful weather:
Fields of gold, and purple heather,
Crimson rose-hips dotting fences,
Orange berries tempting senses,
Yellow beech, and maples fiery,
Creepers red– crowning the scenery!

The sky is rather clearer blue,
The air fresher, and very true;
The sun is gentler, rather yellow,
The moon bigger, soothingly mellow;
The day is neither hot nor cold,
And darker nights– a starry hold!

The robin's haste, the sparrow's twitter,
Fill the air with quite a flutter;
Squirrels run for hoarding nuts,
A fox jumps out behind the huts;
Hares are burrowing deep for winter,
Hedgehogs hunting room for shelter.

In this air of brisk activity,
Farmers have their fair festivity:
Harvest time has come at last,
The moment when their prize is cast.
In fact, it's time we all rejoice–
Bountiful Autumn's left no choice!

12

Winter in England

Winter, thou art ever so *humble,*
Without a show, or a rumble–
The air is hushed, the trees bare,
The grass topped by a frosty layer–
Yet, in a similar image one day,
Christ was born wrapped in hay.

The flakes of snow, do bring down
His note of Unity that does crown
Every feature low or high,
Joining them in a loving tie;
They come pure, and serene,
Making a peaceful, hallowed scene.

Winter also brings festivities,
Simple and childlike activities:
Saint Nicholas and the Christmas tree
And His selfless gifts for free,
And the special winter sunset–
Deepening colours, from the outset.

All aspects of Winter please:
Colourless snow or Christmas trees;
They both bring out that happiness rings
From simple, selfless, natural things.
However, the cold may seem unkind–
But then, Spring is not very far behind!

13

Snowfall

Flakes of purest white
Falling from the sky,
Bring a message of delight
With a compassionate eye:

Pouring down with grace–
A covering crystal pure,
Taking *all* in its embrace–
Making them secure.

It covers the gloomy lane
To make it really bright,
Carrying the mental train
Towards an unseen light.

For when the earth is covered
In the dazzling snow,
Nature is o'erpowered
By a silence that we know:

The air seems quite serene,
There's calmness in the sky,
The earth has hush pristine
And the mind in awe asks why!

A reign of peace prevails
And a message seems to break:
A presence the crystal hails–
O'erwhelming in its make!

My India

14

A Tropical Sunset at Sea

The stage was set for all to see–
A show of lights beside the sea,
The sun making its last decree:
"Get set for my colour spree!"

All at once, the sky turned *gold*
Without a warning to behold–
The tropical sunset, short but bold,
Gripped the mind in a powerful hold.

The golden colour became intense
Which soon gained an *orange* essence;
The sun itself was a glowing presence:
Of *amber* hue in all its brilliance.

The orange light changed to *red,*
Reflecting from the clouds o'erhead
And from the dancing waves it fed:
A fusion of red on a vast spread.

The *fiery* globe kept coming low,
Majestically on the waves below–
Painting *all* in a *crimson* glow
As the finale of the show.

Slowly it journeyed into the ocean,
The waves becoming a *purple* motion.
Sky and water became one portion:
A *blue* curtain of huge proportion.

15

My Dream-India

My type of India exists in my dream,
An ancient land, forlorn and lost it may seem;
Yet, it had a charm that comes from humble living
Which makes a community loving and forgiving,
Since hardship leads to unity and tolerance
And a wish to settle any difference.
Life in my town, was quite tough
With amenities few, and the weather quite rough;
Repairs and field-work, kept the men busy,
Crafts and house-work, kept women dizzy.

My town was quite small, some sixty years ago,
With shops and open fields, on a stone's throw.
There was just one meeting place, the "Chakkar" space,
An abandoned army base, which had lost its trace,
Where weekly markets, sold spices, food and craft,
And shouting vendors, made our ears daft.
It was also the venue for musical shows and festivals
In front of the gods and priestly recitals.
The town had just a single road
Where rickshaws, people and roaming cows strode.

The mile-long road, led from the Chakkar to the Pond:
A water-reserve to the north, ever since its army bond;
Housing and shops lay east of the north-south road,
School, clinic and trees, on the opposite node;
The town was brown, barely a grass to be seen,
Surrounded by crops of the purest green;
The temple was on the western edge of town
Standing on high ground, looking watchfully down,
Facing a patch of sunken land
Where bouts of wrestling used to be planned.

The food was seasonal, grown on local land:
Rice the main food, with chilli at hand;
The water was from the Pond out there,
But boiling it on coal, made us despair;
The summer was harsh, humid and hot,
With monsoonal rains flooding every plot;
The rains would bring havoc everywhere:
Muddy feet, mosquitoes, snakes and flies to bear;
With few oil lamps, and no lamp-posts,
Travel at night saw witches and ghosts.

Hardships were there, but brotherhood existed,
Though life at times seemed daunting and twisted;
People were ready to help each other
And knew how best to work together;
Their simple living, gave quick solutions,
Agreeable to all, with no dissolutions;
A family's grief was shared by all
And help poured in, without a call;
For the children, neighbours were uncle and aunt
And gave the care they could grant.

But things have changed and factories soar,
New faces move in, so trust is no more;
Offices and blocks are common-place
And building-works are at a pace;
The main road now, is a busy thoroughfare
And trucks and lorries race up there.
The tranquil times of brotherly seed
Are now replaced by wealth and greed.
My mind keeps fighting, to reconcile in vain,
And keeps going back, down the memory lane.

16

Seasons in My Sleep

I dream of the seasons I left behind:
The humid high heat of summers of its kind
With torrential rain and clear sunshine,
And welcome warm winters with days fine
When outdoor games would get in line.

My dream's year begins with Holi,
A festival in March, seemingly unholy
As *bhang*[1] is drunk widely as custom
And people dance wildly to a drum
Rubbing *gulaal*[2] on faces in a scrum.

By the end of March, the heat is rising,
The earth browning and cracks arising;
April sees the morning-school start–
Also the time for trees to change their art:
Filling with fruits on their part.

The mango gets hugely scented,
With other fruits no less presented;
The air is filled with their perfumes
And birds move in to show their plumes–
And the song of the cuckoo then resumes.

The full-moon in May, is a glorious sight,
The Earth bathed in its focussed light;
The sky is clear, not a hint of cloud,
The shining Moon: majestic and proud,
Declaring its reign clear and loud.

---

[1] An intoxicating drink

[2] Dry coloured powder

June ushers the mighty Monsoon
Which dominates the Summer like a tycoon:
Powerful, potent, pitiless and preposterous,
Yet gentle, genuine, genial and generous,
Without which, no harvest would be sonorous.

The start of the Monsoon, is a sight of wonder,
Announcing presence with loudest thunder,
Pouring for days on the parched earth,
Trying to prove its real worth,
Giving the farmers awe and mirth.

Autumn brings the festivals in swing
With Divali having the final sling;
This Festival of Lights, is the most colourful,
With presents exchanged in plentiful,
And sweets made by the bucketful.

The winter months remain the most pleasant
When pretty blooms fill every crescent;
The gentle clime sets children free,
Playing around the banyan tree–
And elders watch, to soak up the glee.

These are the seasons I see at night
When during the day I've lost their sight;
And their visitations will not cease
Since they seem to have a lease
Which goes beyond mortal peace.

17

The Burst of The Monsoon

With the grass as dry as hay
During the month of May,
The earth is parched with gaping cracks,
Obviously missing the water it lacks.
With mercury climbing steadily,
Around forty Celsius readily,
The afternoons are unbearably hot
And work is naturally suffering a lot.
The sky is clear and blue,
With no hope of a change or clue
As to when the heat would abate,
With not a mist or cloud to date!

But now it's June, and the Monsoon arrives
To crush the oppressive Sun's drives;
It comes bouncing to deride
The menacing Sun's ego and pride.
"Out of the blue and shunning a pause,
Closer and closer the Monsoon draws–
Wearing the thickest coat of cloud,
Riding a chariot making it proud:
The thundering chariot swirling round,
Storming through with deafening sound,
Announcing war in loudest highs,
With armour flashing across the skies!"

The sky goes black as charred cakes
From which a mighty laughter breaks
To say the Monsoon has o'er-run
The powers of the mighty Sun.
It starts raining with generosity
To undo the Sun's atrocity:
It pours and pours without a break
With drops as big as a Rupee's make.
The whole day and the whole night
It rains and rains with all its might,
The Monsoon thus fulfilling indeed
Its promise to help at times of need!

But villagers are in disarray,
Wondering if it got carried away
And so o'erdid its helping hand,
The village flooded on each strand!
The pond has simply vanished from sight,
With neighbouring fields in similar plight;
Boats are plying everywhere,
Helping people to move from there.
Slowly they move to higher ground:
To the old school compound;
For three whole days, they live in fear,
And only then, conditions clear!

Childhood Days

18

Childhood Days

I remember childhood days,
With its dreamy, care-free ways–
Heedless how I moved around,
Mindless how the world went round:

A child resides in fantasy–
The pirates and their piracy;
To draw attention to oneself,
One has to be the child itself.

I remember parents' care
And how I sought them everywhere–
Often I ignored school
To be within their loving pool:

A young child needs to be secure–
Secure in love and feel for sure;
If this warmth is denied,
The child's confidence will subside.

I remember dad's scolding
With an eye to children's grounding–
He would firmly point my failing
If I ever made wrong sailing:

Children need to be guided along
On what is right and what is wrong,
And learn to make responsible plan–
The child being the father of man.

19

Books

Books have been my oldest friend
In every form of life's bend;
Solace and joy– a book can lend,
Which *can* enhance natural trend.

Books enclose the minds of the dead,
Great authors who have gone ahead,
Whose brilliance can easily be read
And in our lives, their values spread.

Books are the records of the Earth,
A store of all that is of worth
Ever since mankind took birth–
And so for books, there is no dearth:

They contain the human culture,
Earliest forms of Scripture,
All the arts and architecture,
And every scientific literature.

Books can have personal appeal,
Much more than TV can reel:
They *can* remove the lonesome feel
And be a friend with a lifelong deal.

Hence, books can alter people's nature,
Can transform social structure,
Give a nation, new stature,
Lead mankind to a glorious future!

20

The Examinee

Trembling like a leaf,
Pale with grief,
With pulse on a beat,
He creeps to his seat.

There's no loud groan
But inner moan
In the Exam Hall
Awaiting the Master's call.

The Master warns by speech
Of rules not to breach;
He then spells the time
When the end will chime.

The clock is thumping by,
Matching the heart's cry;
A cruel crow caws to convey:
"It's a damn, dismal day!"

Papers are taken round,
Silence to a pin-drop sound:
Time for the last prayer
Before the Questions flare.

Two full hours to come
Of sheer sickening scum;
And youth just fails to tell:
Why this hideous horrid hell!

21

A Young Boy's Wish

I want to help my Gran who is old–
Finest lady, whose life has gone cold;
I'd like to help her with her shopping,
Take her out, where birds are hopping;
I wish she moves to where I roam
Instead of the far old people's home.

I remember, how in younger years,
She used to care, and wipe my tears;
She was my playmate during holidays,
And my guide in so many ways,
Since my parents had a shop
And their work would never stop.

Studies and extras of a huge range,
Take up my time, which I can't change;
But on Sundays, I could reach her,
Sit and talk and eat with her,
And in this way, make her share
A word or two, with one who'd care.

It doesn't seem wise for me to wait,
Since it could be much too late;
She has to be given a preference,
And this would make a difference:
Elders need love, as much as we do,
And helping them out, could help us too.

22

True Education

Education is the passing on of culture
From one to the next generation:
All that's dear to mankind's nature
And all the rules of self-elevation.
Education prepares for every season–
A *balanced* man, with powers to reason.

Education should make a virtuous man,
With all round wit, to tackle a problem;
And moral courage to stick to a plan
To help all those, who are in mayhem.
Education has a wide span:
It doesn't just make a knowledgeable man.

True education gives *depth* of wisdom
Making one sensitive to others' suffering,
With knowledge that we live in a kingdom
Joined to each other, in a beautiful offering.
We are *not* islands in isolation,
But are linked in true relation.

And *kindness* is the foremost quality
Which they should aim to teach,
Showing the unity in diversity
And the ties we must not breach:
Awareness of unity, is essential
If *education* is to find its potential.

War

23

A Soldier's Dream-Maiden

After a hard day's battle,
Huddled into barracks like cattle,
She sees me in my dreams,
From which a ray of joy beams
And lights me up with a charm,
Pushing aside the day's alarm.

She has a smile just for me,
Drawing me close for me to see:
The fairest maiden,
With hair gold-laden,
And eyes so blue–
A beauty rare and true.

Her hair is long and curly,
Teeth are white and pearly;
The skin has glossy sheen,
A marble form, rarely seen–
The colour is peach and cream,
Fulfilling my cherished dream.

Her lips are red and cosy,
Cheeks are pink and rosy;
The figure is tall and slender,
To which I totally surrender;
Her eyes are shy but sure,
Whose aim– I can't endure!

She is the lovers' starry night,
The crimson rose of warm delight,
The shyful deer with eager eye,
A lightning flash across the sky.
She is, to me, the living thread
And all the rest are simply dead.

She will soon be coming along,
And it can't be much too long
Before she comes to lift the veil
Of fear, guns, and its trail–
Changing the day's gruesome sails,
And take me to, where love prevails.

24

A Soldier at Sixteen

A soldier at sixteen
Is ever so keen
To go to battle
Where cannons rattle.

The aim to get drafted,
Their peers had crafted:
To be the gem,
A hero amongst them!

They scarce realise
It's not at all wise
To toy with the gun,
Which can well stun.

In battle, it kills
And blood spills–
Limbs mutilate,
Necks decapitate.

And then these boys
Lose all their joys
On being shell-shocked–
And hang in rooms locked.

But is it in the morals
To paint rich laurels
And lure young chums
With trumpets and drums?

25

A Soldier's Dilemma

From the drab and muddy trenches,
Filled with logs, serving as benches,
We could see our line of soldiers
Moving up the mighty boulders
Acting as their shields from foe
Who were ruthless top to toe.

A hundred made our fighting prime
While in trenches we marked time:
To emerge when they demanded
Just in case they were stranded.
We kept a watch for their call,
Lest their pride should hurt and fall.

A leafy dense forested ridge
Acted as a natural bridge
Between us and the enemy ranks
Hiding under guised camps.
We lay in wait for them to urge
When we'd make an onward surge.

A mighty wind came through the trees
Blowing down a chilling freeze.
Then, one by one, helmets appeared
On the ridge as black dust cleared.
Then they headed straight for us:
A gory battle started thus.

For one full hour, the guns were fired;
Heads kept rolling, till both sides tired.
The boom of guns was quite enough
To make the devil call off its bluff.
So they fell back, beyond the hills
Leaving us to count the kills.

The guns had just silenced themselves
To be replaced by groaning selves.
There were cries of "Help!" all over,
Gaping wounds without a cover!
The place was littered with men in pain,
Helmets strewn on the bloodied plain.

There were bodies without a head,
Some without limbs, and some half-dead.
We, who were whole, looked on and cried,
And the value of fighting, seemed to slide.
Half of the injured were our men,
The other half from enemy's den.

We couldn't sit back, and watch the sight
And let our conscience have a bite;
We gathered all, from near and wide,
Including those from enemy's side,
And tried our best to ease their pain–
Wondering if we fought in vain.

Lessons from Animals

26

My Pet

They say you have passed away,
And yet your eyes are gazing at me to say
"My love is around, so don't shed tears
As love is not counted in years:
I will be there for you for ever
As long as the stars have light to deliver."

We never conversed with any word,
But words would be so absurd
In expressing pure love which is silent,
Whose experience makes the soul vibrant:
Your look of devotion, and loving commotion,
Was always enough, for highest elation.

There never was a nobler soul than you
With such commitment, and demands so few:
Your utter and *selfless* devotion,
Will always be my inspiration.
You were true to your noble creed–
Man's best friend at times of need.

Through your example, I hope, I will one day
Spread your love to each and everyone that stay
Around me in my modest circle of living,
And spread your light of loving–
The love that you taught me with such passion:
Caring with humbleness, without expectation.

27

Lessons from Animals

Animals have the finest virtues–
Exemplary and most thoughtful;
And if we care to heed their clues,
Our lives would be so meaningful:

See the dog's faithfulness
In its loving eyes,
Guarding with humbleness
Whether it lives or dies.

The cat points to cleanliness
When it washes with its paws;
"Cleanliness is Godliness"–
It's saying without a pause.

The spider shows tenacity,
Building its web in rain–
Working with audacity,
Fighting every pain.

The toil of the humming bees
Collecting honey for its creed,
Remind us never to ease
Our efforts for a noble deed.

The ant is a tireless warrior–
Climbing the steepest hill,
Its size is not a barrier
Against its deepest will.

The crow, having found some feed,
Hates to have the lot;
And so it caws to bring its creed,
And loves a shared pot.

The squirrel saves for winter days:
Nuts of chosen texture,
Which has lessons for our ways
In planning for the future.

The elephant knows its helper–
Never lets kindness go in vain:
It will never harm its keeper,
Even if it goes quite insane.

The clever fox uses its brain
To plan a multiple vent,
Foreseeing hunters and their train
Would raid it with intent.

The nest by tender swallow
For its nestlings' childhood,
Says love must never be shallow
And points to true parenthood.

Then there is the pairing dove
With its message of pure love–
Should one ever fail to thrive,
The other refuses to survive!

28

Fair Butterfly

How I commend
What you display
And the message
You convey!

Your slender body,
The folding wings,
And brilliant colours–
Remind of good things.

Without your flutter,
A garden is bare;
The flower you kiss,
Has a lucky share.

Besides sheer beauty,
You do signify
What we can achieve,
Should we try.

Once a worm,
A caterpillar:
Thin and plain,
A mere wriggler.

But, you built a cocoon
To shut the world out,
Therein to scheme
The form to sprout.

You won your prize,
All else outclassed;
With sheer will,
Barriers you passed.

Once you were helpless
As all worms are,
But now you have wings
To take you far.

Transformed you are
As all can see,
Proving to them:
Strength is in thee.

We have to reach
Our latent powers,
That wait in us
To burst in showers.

29

The Zoo Animal

My body is made of gold
And has a golden mane,
Which they all behold
But no one sees my pain.

They say I am strong–
The king and mightiest animal!
But then they are so wrong
Since my life is minimal.

I used to run and glide,
Beat the wind with my stride,
Roll on grass, jump and slide
With the members of my pride.

But they used every trick
And laid a wily snare–
To earn themselves a prized pick
And trap me and scare.

Now I have no choice–
Imprisoned in a cell;
With not a say or voice,
I await death knell.

Can't anyone come and offer
To lift me from this pain?
Must you make me suffer
And watch my tears in vain?

30

The Caged Bird

I'm a caged bird
Without a choice
To move around
Or have a voice.

And here you come
To wish "Good day!"
But what to say
With life at bay.

I wish to swap
Positions with you,
And then to ask
"How well are you?"

I miss my flights,
My kin, my land,
My favourite sights
On sea and sand.

How would you like
Your moves all tied,
Forced in a cell
Locked from outside?

Give me my right:
The right to be free,
Which is the same
For you and for me.

31

The Bird's Faith

I've trained myself to glide,
So I can float at will with pride
And have a confidence that will hold,
Leaving me free to behold:

Nature's beautiful lakes and forests,
The rapid falls from mountain crests,
Rolling waves and curled wavelets,
Colourful sunrise and sunsets.

I also watch the morning rush-hour
And the vast commuter shower:
Flooding into buses, in such hurry
With faces frowned, showing great worry!

But I, for one, have nothing to worry–
With simple needs, I don't scurry;
I live in the present, without duress
And leave it to Nature, to take on stress.

I take from Nature what I need
And leave the rest for others to feed;
I have no quest for hoarding and greed,
And share the world with all my creed:

Should we follow Nature's harmony,
Sharing things and shunning greed,
There'll be no stress or agony–
Provision enough for mankind's need.

32

Going Along With Nature

"Oh Wind!", they grumble,
But I can make them humble:
Make a castle tumble,
Create lightning and rumble.

Typhoon and storm are my game
Which you cannot dare to tame;
I can bring anyone to shame
Tampering with my name and fame.

I must warn those who ignore
My real strength, which is much more,
For I can shatter every door
And shake the Earth to its core!

Yet, I'm the force in all windmills
Which are placed on windy hills;
To them I help gain the skills,
Since their plans match my wills:

You have to go along my taste,
And to my liking, make things chaste;
But, if you act in reckless haste,
Your plans will *always* go to waste.

So, when the sea is really rough
And the pessimist calls it tough,
Adjusting the sails, can be enough:
Going along with Nature's huff.

33

Two Silly Goats

In the thick of forest-land
With nothing but creepers at hand
And leafy trees standing high
With branches right across the sky,
Two silly goats were in stride
Full of ego and full of pride
Towards an ageing natural bridge
Made by a tree blown off a ridge.

They approached from opposite sides
With murky light and mist besides:
A howling wind whistled to say
That perils may befall their way.
The bridge spanned a gorge most awful:
Deep and rocky, and most dreadful,
But the goats felt most sure-footed
And, in their arrogance, blindly strutted.

They jumped without viewing,
From opposites sides– collision ensuing.
They faced each other with a frown
And neither of them would back down;
A fight broke out lacking foresight,
The bridge swaying from left to right;
They made rude gesture, pointing finger,
Forgetting danger, fraught with anger.

The haughty goats just slipped and fell
Into the gorge in darkest hell.
They had allowed emotions to rule
And these, in turn, made them a fool!
The mist then cleared and the sun came out,
And birds and goats were up and about;
And from their midst, two gentle goats,
Decided to roam, singing notes.

Without realising, and looking no further,
They sprang on the bridge to face each other
The goats could neither move forwards
Nor could they possibly move backwards,
For the bridge seemed much too slender
And moving backwards would be a blunder.
But they were gentle, polite and humble
With no wish for hassle and rumble.

So they sat down, to think and discuss,
Without any quarrel, or any fuss;
A simple compromise found their favour:
One would crouch, the other crawl over.
Thus the two goats managed to mask
A near-enough impossible task,
Giving a lesson, simple but tall:
United we stand, divided we fall.

34

The Hare and The Tortoise

A haughty hare, hurtful and hateful,
Loved to give the tortoise a mouthful:
"O you snoring slumbering slag,
Most boring, blundering brag."

The tortoise couldn't take any more,
Left the lake, and came ashore:
"Why you troubling me all day
When I've never crossed your way?

"I could be your real friend,
For I have qualities that could send
Joy to you with my kindness,
Patience, tolerance and humbleness."

But the hare's thinking was low,
Driven by his vast ego;
He just harboured bullying taste,
And so went on to say with haste:

"Race with me to the opposite shore–
To that tree where creepers soar,
And prove to me: you're not sluggish,
Or else admit: you're most rubbish."

Over-confidence for the win,
Was responsible for this din:
He saw it as a golden chance
To enjoy a boastful dance!

The race began in all earnest,
Both contestants doing their best–
The hare galloping in his drill,
The tortoise using every skill.

The morning had a soothing breeze,
Inspiring the mood to be at ease;
Yet the two kept slogging on
In the golden sun of dawn.

Soon the hare was much ahead,
And when he saw how far he led,
He felt he could afford a break–
Perhaps a rest beside the lake!

The cool air, around the water,
Relaxed his mind in every quarter;
Soon the hare was fast asleep
And lost his chances in the deep.

When the hare opened his eyes,
He felt like bursting into cries:
The tortoise hailed the winning line,
And he could only watch and pine.

The hare's ego was to blame
Which put his talents into shame;
Ego, haughtiness and self-pride
Had pushed his thinking to the side.

35

The Lion and The Mouse

A mighty lion became ambitious,
Ruling the forest, in ways most vicious–
His aim being to crush all creatures,
Regardless of their creed or features.

He wanted all, to pay him homage–
Submit to his repressive image;
He planned to round up any rebellion–
Sparing not, even one in a million!

But a tiny mouse became very anxious
And thought the lion was being noxious;
It argued that all mice were free
And did not need a new decree!

At this, the lion roared in temper,
Making the mouse run and scamper.
And so the lion ruled far and near,
The forest freezing in fright and fear!

But then a hunter was on a quest
Who wanted his prize to be the best:
And so he set up a lion-trap–
Of green strings in a grass-wrap.

As soon as the lion came out of his den,
He stepped on the net which curled then;
The more he struggled, the more it tangled,
And kept on tightening, the more he wrangled.

The lion roared in grief and despair,
But no one came to his rescue there–
Scared of his wicked nature,
Frightened of his vile stature.

At last, he saw the mouse around
Which saw the lion tightly bound;
He begged for help, and cried in tears,
The mouse seeing the lion's fears.

The mouse took pity on the beast
And swallowed pride to say the least:
With sharpest teeth, it cut the strings,
And the lion could see what unity brings!

The lion was forced to think and pause
On the damage arrogance can cause;
He couldn't believe, he'd be so helpless,
Begging to a mouse, seemingly powerless!

Selfishness was proved to be wrong
And vanity crushed not before long:
The mouse is as useful as any on Earth,
Unique in its role, unique in its worth.

All have a part to play in the Whole,
Be it the elephant, or the mole;
Even the tiniest is worth in gold,
Completing Nature's *balanced* hold.

36

The Donkey Ride

There was once an ageing merchant
Who lived in a blistering desert land;
He had a young and lively grandson
Skilled to ride their donkey on sand.

It was the close of trade that day–
A great day's sale at the bazaar,
When spices sold like hot kebab
As though buyers had gone bizarre.

The man was happy with the sales
As also the boy who had the chance
To watch the fluted snake-charmer,
A cockerel-fight and a monkey-dance.

Since all the spices had been sold
The donkey would go light on load,
The old man asked the boy to ride
To spare him of the blazing road.

So they began their journey home
In brightest red and airy sunset,
Rejoicing in their day's success
And singing loudly from the outset.

However, as they travelled along,
Some people's looks went oddly cold;
And one of them came out quite loud:
"How come, the boy ignores the old?"

At this, the boy came down to ground
And begged his granddad take the ride;
But soon they were to be surprised
As passers-by were quick to chide.

They joked how selfish he could be
Taking an airy donkey ride,
And ignore a helpless child
Trying to foot the desert wide.

And so the man pulled up the boy
Hoping to calm the crowd at least;
But onlookers were most upset
Saying the load would kill the beast.

Both of them came down the animal–
In confusion, walked beside it;
But the mob were quick to mock them
Asking why no one would ride it.

The old man panicked– in despair,
Thought there was but one solution:
That to carry the wretched donkey
With the strongest resolution.

They tied the donkey's legs in pairs,
Hung it, head down, from a holder
Which was just a bamboo rod
Made to rest on their shoulder.

Seeing the animal hanging thus,
The people laughed, and made great fun;
The man shuddered and gave a cry,
Then left the beast, and made a run!

Thus the pet, lost its master,
And the trader, lost its porter;
A journey, which began with laughter,
Ended in total disaster.

The burning sand, a journey long,
A hard day's toil, and the mocking throng–
Pushed them to do another wrong:
To follow an unknown route along.

At last, they reached home late at night,
Both of them in a pitiable plight;
Grandma couldn't believe the sight:
She thought they had a nasty fight.

They lied the donkey died for good,
But she uncovered the coined falsehood;
She then screamed as much as she could,
And they were shocked, as anyone would!

So the man, and his grandson,
Lost the day when it was won:
All their triumphs were undone
Though their goods had sold like bun.

The man ignored his common-sense
And foolishly kept himself so tense;
Since he followed others' guidance,
They took advantage of his innocence:

It's simple folly, to appease all,
For those who do, just meet their fall:
One should weigh up the job's demand,
And then follow one's *own* command.

Stories

37

The Loyal Scarecrow

I stand in the middle of the field,
Below the sky without a shield,
Bracing every kind of weather,
Be it wind and snow together,
Guarding my Master's cherished field,
Or else the crows would take its yield.

Silent, as the stars above me,
Fixed, as the hills around me,
I stand in muted firmness,
Pushing his harvest to its fullness–
Working *alone*, night and day,
Because I scare all friends away.

My clothes are not at all snobbish–
O'er-size coat with breeches rubbish,
With a cap on coat, sown in a hurry
Since my Master was in a flurry.
Yet I wear them with humility,
Surrendering all, to servility.

Neglected though I am at present,
I remain his loyal servant:
My devotion shall bring gratitude,
Drive my Lord to lift my solitude,
For no heart can show much fortitude
Against a humble, patient servitude.

38

A Lover's Emotion

Her first love,
Her only love,
Has been late
At her date.

It was an hour
By the clock-tower
Over vowed time
At the last chime.

As the clock counts,
Her worry mounts;
She feels sick
And panics quick:

"Has he changed,
With me estranged?
Did he forget
The vows he set?

"Or, could it be
That it's me
Who couldn't impress
And hence this mess?"

Self-hate reels
And she feels:
She is worthless
And so useless!

Yet the clock pounds
Its brutal rounds;
And peace crumbles
As hope tumbles.

Emotions rise
And patience dies:
A minute's wait
Seems years too late.

Choked by emotion
Defying proportion,
She cries at heart
As hopes depart.

Her rolling tears
Show her fears:
He won't turn up,
He's given her up!

She feels dejected,
Cruelly rejected.
With fears linking,
She is sinking!

Her only will
With pulse at nil
Is to be there
Where angels fare:

"O, come sweet Death,
And take my breath
To thine own peace
Where sorrows cease."

No Juliet lives
If Romeo gives
A cold look to say:
"I leave you away."

So she has fallen–
Crushed and sullen,
With one last plea
To crows and flea:

"When I am dead
Eat body and head
But take my eyes
To the skies.

"For them to see
The cherry tree
Where we vowed
To make love proud."

But now her love
Who was late
Is at her gate
When it's far too late.

39

The King, The Priest and The Lion

There was once an arrogant king,
Whose presence gave a chilling ring;
He had made it very plain:
"Anyone against him, would be slain."
There was also a priestly man,
Gentle and kind to all his clan.
Once, while tending plants he had sown,
He heard a most distressing groan,
Coming from outside his grounds,
Whining mixed with gasping sounds.
Being compassionate, and so kind,
He set out into the woods to find
A lion lying in despair
Nursing a thigh with an arrow in there.
The hunting taste of the cruel king,
Was to blame for this terrible thing!
At first, the lion made him freeze,
But a second look, put him at ease:
The lion was most terribly etched,
Begging for help, with leg stretched.
Seeing the wound, he couldn't refrain,
Pulled out the arrow, relieving pain.
He could see the lion's relief,
For it stood in disbelief!
Then it turned and moved away–
And through the woods, made its way.

Upon returning, the priest told friends
About the king's hunting trends;
But his friends gossiped much,
The news reaching the king as such.
The king went mad to say the least
Resolving to punish the innocent priest.
He devised a plan to kill:
To push the priest against his will
To face a lion in a ring
While he himself would watch and sing!
It was now the king's birthday,
And candles were lit along the way;
And a hungry lion waited to see
Who its fair meal would be!
But soon it was clear from the lion's sigh,
That this was just a friendly tie:
The lion gazed at the priest's eye,
The priest seeing the scarred thigh.
The lion went low, as though to greet
And started kissing the priest's feet.
The king couldn't believe his eyes
And wanted to know the background ties;
He learnt about the priest and the arrow,
And was filled with shame and sorrow:
He thought the priest had shown the way
That love and kindness wins the day.

40

The Golden Touch

A greedy king wanted more money,
So, at the temple, offered sweets and honey
And knelt on his knees, as the custom of old,
Begging for riches in diamonds and gold!

His vigil at the temple, went on for days,
And he wasn't prepared to change his ways;
So, the Lord appeared to him at night
And asked the reason for his plight.

The king replied that his pundits say:
"The Lord gives in, if you bargain your way."
So I've come, to plead for more wealth
While I take care, of your temple's health:

"I'll put your idol on a raised table,
And the temple painted, by workers most able;
It will have gardens and flowers in ample,
And will have fences, so herds can't trample."

The Lord smiled and looked at his eyes
And asked him to choose, and be very wise:
"Have the chance to serve the old,
Or have the touch that bears gold."

The king preferred the golden choice,
Hoping he could then rejoice;
And so he gained powers to mould:
Whatever he touched, turned into gold!

The king was so happy to test his powers,
Thanking the Lord for His kind showers
Until he was served his kingly dishes
Which turned to gold without his wishes!

The king wasn't able to eat his meal,
So ran to the temple, to change his deal;
He begged the Lord to remove the touch
And tried to bargain and offer much.

The Lord appeared and blessed him so,
As he had learnt his lesson to know
That worldly wants without a need,
Lead to suffering which they feed.

Too much wealth can sow the seed
Which can encourage pain to breed–
For happiness lies in lying low,
In modest living, without a show.

41

Raaju's Birthday

Ten-year-old Raaju's birthday was quite near,
But, where it would be celebrated, was not clear;
So he went up to his Dad to find out,
And learnt that his Mum was still down with gout;
So the temple would have to be booked in haste
Where meals were pricey, but of the finest taste!

Though sad for his Mum, Raaju felt elated
That his birthday would still be celebrated;
He kept dreaming how he would sit with friends
And laugh and joke and eat till the evening ends.
Soon the day came close, and he had a call
From his Dad, to go and book the temple hall.

The Dad gave him a coin most brilliant-looking
To be given to the priest for the temple-booking.
With the coin on the table, Raaju prepared to go,
But his sister was curious about the coin's glow;
The boy replied, "The coin is a magical one
And that, if planted, would glow like the Sun!"

So, as he was getting ready, she ran to the field
And sowed the coin, to see its yield;
But a pauper boy, was watching all this outside
And took the coin, when the little girl went inside.
Raaju found the coin had vanished from the table
And that his sister had sown it, to test his fable!

They rushed outside to dig up and see,
But the coin wasn't there to give them glee.
Raaju's father had no more coins to give
And Raaju had himself to blame or forgive!
His dream-birthday had met his worst fears,
And his birthday friends were now his own tears.

Raaju had learnt the hard way
That making up tales, ruins the day;
Though he had told the simplest of lies,
Still it proved to be unwise:
Belief in lying, must be a fallacy–
Honesty being the best policy.

42

A Bedtime Story

Shooting stars can go astray
And one of them can come your way;
And such a star, from the skies,
Has just entered your sleepy eyes;
And to find where it could be,
You have to close your eyes to see.

Within your eyes you will see
A hundred gems on a tree;
And near its roots, upon the ground,
A shining ball, rolling around.
This is your *shooting star,* of good size,
Sent to you from fairies, as your prize.

As you'll see, the ball is fit
For one like you to ride and sit;
It's quite soft and yet strong,
And has a mind that never went wrong:
It can take off, into the skies,
If you can ask the ball to rise.

So, try your luck, to get on
This magical star from Renkon
Which is the kingdom of fairies
"Fond of sweets from milk dairies".
If you can just remember this clue,
You can please them through and through.

Yes! You decide to ride the ball,
And off it goes, above trees so tall;
Up and up you go along
Into the skies with a song;
Look around as you glide
And so enjoy the starry ride.

But look! Where you've come to land,
Where everything is simply grand;
Girls with wings are looking on:
These are the fairies of Renkon;
Their elves are dressed in uniform
As though warfare, is their norm.

The grass is much greener than green,
And it has a glossy sheen;
The sky is much bluer than blue
Against the clouds, so white and true.
The hills around have every flower,
Surrounding the beautiful castle tower:

The tower has gems of every fold,
Dazzling with beauty quite untold;
The castle puts your breath on hold
With windows made of purest gold;
The jewelled doors stand out bold
Against the walls with carvings old!

The place is like a treasure hold,
A stunning sight to behold!
But, watch out! The elves have rolled
From their fields, with faces cold.
They seem to head with lips scrolled
Towards yourself in an angry mould!

So pull out, before they come:
They seem so rude, and fearsome.
They wouldn't be your mate or chum,
So get rolling from their hum.
But what hard luck! The ball seems dumb,
As it has gone totally numb!

So there isn't any way out,
Nor would the elves listen to your shout.
"Then, take some sweets from your pocket
And throw them hard at their locket.
Sweets made from milk dairies
Soothe all pixies, elves and fairies."

They now quieten their guns and hums,
And welcome you with pipes and drums!
Your star, too, is now alive,
So you can stay, or take a drive.
But, isn't it strange
That simple sweets could make the change?

43

The Weird Old Sisters

Dancing round the cauldron fire,
We enjoy murky desire:
Casting round evil spell,
Driving people into hell.
We follow the devil's bark,
Being sisters of the dark.

Look! Who is this in Robes of Gold,
Looking for a Selfish hold?
Upon this fool, our spell will work,
Let's trap this worthless quirk.
We can play upon his Greed,
Twist and turn his noble creed.

We'll flare up his hidden Ambition,
Tempting him on a murderous mission
From which there is no turning back
With enemies hounding him in a pack:
To cover-up for his heinous crime,
He'll be butchering all the time.

The spate of killings, will breed insanity–
Drive him to its doomed calamity.
The world has been unfair to us
And we will not spare them thus:
They mistook us for a joke
And we shall burn them into smoke.

44

The Golden Eggs

To her surprise, the lady found
Her goose laid eggs of a shiny mould;
At first she couldn't believe her eyes
But then the jeweller proved it gold!

The eggs were made of purest gold–
Solid gold of so much worth;
And soon the lady began to think:
She'd be the richest on this Earth.

She saw herself decked in pearls,
Her house with marble on the floor–
And windows made of golden frames,
With gems on knobs of every door.

Then a plan seized her mind
Which could make her rich o'ernight:
To get all eggs in just one go
By slitting the goose's belly outright.

But when she cut the goose open,
She couldn't find any egg to take;
And to her great dismay and grief,
She lost a dream of royal make!

Wealth beyond need is destructive
Since it rouses endless craving,
Greed is always ill-constructive
Bearing actions quite depraving.

45

Compassion

Once, a young son wanted his share–
So the father gave, what he could spare;
The son then left for a distant land,
Imagining life would be so grand.

But he was young and immature,
Seeking pleasures quite impure;
He soon squandered all his share
And no one came to his rescue there.

He tried to do some lowly jobs,
But was met with bullying mobs;
Hunger wanted him to return,
Though his pride raised concern.

However, his health hustled him home,
Regretting why he vowed to roam.
With a sorrowful face, and a head in shame,
He stood at the gate, with himself to blame.

But, all these years, the father lay in worry
Since he knew, his son was bred in luxury
And hence would find it hard to cope
If things did go against his hope.

So, when he saw his son's face,
Every suffering he could trace–
His compassion shunned limitation,
Forgiving his son without hesitation.

Miscellaneous

46

Music

Music is the voice of Nature–
Harmony being its feature–
For music is pure harmony,
Reflecting Nature's symphony:
Acclaiming unity, denouncing fear,
Bringing peace and spreading cheer.

Music is for one and all,
Making no distinction at all–
The notes carry universal appeal,
Stirring emotions in their feel,
Charging the air towards a trend,
Driving thought towards an end:

The power of music is well known–
How it can change a battle's tone,
Charm a snake and make it low,
Lift a plant and make it grow,
How it can make a glass dissolve,
And change a sinking man's resolve!

Mixed with morals, music can turn
And firmly help, to return
The straying soul to its goal:
Towards its real unified role;
And so create a brotherhood of man,
Advancing joy on a truly wide span.

47

Paradise on Earth

Within our grasp, there is a land
Where love and kindness are at hand–
Where everyone does understand
That separateness cannot stand:
A sense of unity ties the land,
Which runs across every strand.

The sunshine is of purest gold,
Embracing all, in a loving hold;
The sky is true to pledges old,
Sheltering all, without being told;
The air is gentle, never cold,
Blowing sweetness from its fold.

The moon gives out a song at night–
The song of love, beaming delight,
Covering all, in silvery light:
Cool, relaxing, dashing fright,
Proving to all, that love is right,
For it can bring joy in sight.

This is the land, waiting to be found
Where peace and happiness just abound,
Where humility holds the ground
And compassion tunes the sound:
The land is well within our bound
If we could simply turn around.

48

True Beauty

Beauty can be a bed of roses,
Or just a lawn, in green poses;
It can be a colourful sunset,
Or a colourless snow-carpet.

It can be a roaring waterfall,
Or a silent lake, beside mountain tall;
It can be the dazzling brook at noon,
Or the night sky, with the floating moon.

Beauty can also be a novel or a book,
Or a fancied castle with a fanciful look;
It can be a meal, eaten alfresco,
Or a night-out, at a modern disco.

So, beauty can have different faces:
Things that please the mood and senses;
But such things have a fleeting charm–
Can bring in craving, causing harm.

Yet, there are virtues, one can cite,
That are beauties, in their own right:
They aren't subjective to any season,
And not related to mood and reason.

The virtues of sacrifice, and being kind,
Serve as beauties, for *all* mankind–
Spreading peace and joy *forever*
To both the receiver and the giver.

49

The Unity of Nature

All things around us, are united–
Animals, plants and everything sighted;
A simple study will make it clear
That unity reigns far and near:

Every matter attracts another,
Gravity pulling them together;
And, for every type of action,
There is a balanced twin reaction.

Plants make food to keep alive,
Which also helps animals survive;
And they, in turn, provide the elements
Used by plants to make the nutriments.

Withered bodies die and decay,
Which fertilize fields, and make way
For young saplings to succeed,
Making life's cycle proceed.

Seas vaporise to give us rain
Which runs back to the sea to drain;
So, *all* things do integrate,
And are meant to so relate.

With its balanced, peaceful unity,
Nature keeps its pristine beauty;
But, if we shun its unified theme,
We *will* destroy its elegant sheen.

50

My Daughter's Always on the Phone

My daughter's always on the phone,
Chatting in a bubbly tone:
Sometimes laughing, sometimes giggling,
Often joking and then chuckling–
Mostly crouching, seldom walking,
She is always doing her talking,
All the hours of the day,
Be it August, June or May.

She holds the phone ever so tight,
Be it day, or be it night–
Is always ready to have a fight
Should someone question her right;
And if anyone dares to snatch,
Like a cat, she does scratch.
My daughter's always on the phone,
Chatting in a bubbly tone.

I keep asking why she phones–
A million reasons she adorns:
School-work for the coming Mock,
She is working in her talk!
"Dad, homework in every zone
Is better sorted on the phone."
My daughter's always on the phone,
Chatting in a bubbly tone.

But, who is at the other end,
Pushing the house round the bend?
It can't be anyone else but him:
That creaky, croaky, creepy Jim!
I wish they ring the marriage bell
And leave the phone for us to yell.
My daughter's always on the phone,
Chatting in a bubbly tone.

Yet, there could be another cause
Tapping her mind without a pause.
Perhaps we need to lend an ear
To show that she is close and dear–
Then she'll be inclined to us
And will freely talk and discuss.
My daughter's always on the phone,
Chatting in a bubbly tone.

Her teachers think: she wants attention,
And they are tired of giving detention.
They doubt if she would ever pass
Unless she concentrates in class
And makes a change to impress
At listening more and talking less.
My daughter's always on the phone
Chatting in a bubbly tone.

51

The Position of Women

Women are the Soul of the Earth,
To whom humanity owes its birth;
They have the caring, motherly make–
To give up their needs, for other's sake.

Yet, some communities value them less
And place them under a man's prowess,
Assuming they can't cope beyond home
Or beyond a simple shopping roam.

But any test could prove their excellence,
Creative powers and intelligence;
Numerous women have made their mark
With their natural, inner spark:

Versed in the language of the heart,
Women excel in music, poetry and art–
They have patience and resilience,
Attributes for innovative brilliance.

Women make up half the nation–
Ignoring them, locks a huge portion:
A loss of half the nation's potential,
A heavy price for being partial.

Give the respect women deserve,
Treating them in equal nerve;
Then the world would happier be,
And each nation– a prosperous tree.

52

The Wife's Complaint

Your wild addiction
For poem and verse,
Has thrown the house
Into reverse!

Day in, day out,
Sitting in vain–
Beard overgrown
Like an insane.

A couch-potato
Is what you'll be–
Unhealthy tramp,
A sight to see.

I just don't see
How these silly verse,
Can be of worth
To fill the purse.

With time so wasted,
Income will fly;
With nothing to eat,
Your poems I'll fry.

Come off that chair
And lift your cramp,
Before I come
And smash the lamp!

53

Confidence

Whether we succeed or fail
Depends on how strong or frail
We are in our *own* perception
Of our planning and its inception:

Schemes reluctantly started
And faith in it only half-hearted,
Are doomed from their very beginning
With never a chance of winning:

A real belief is vital,
Not just oral recital,
Since belief gives birth to real zest,
Making us lend our very best.

And for a self-confident man,
Prepared to do whatever he can,
Nature with its resources delves:
God helps those who help themselves.

And what if we fail at any time?
We must look up to the next chime;
A setback should bring no recess:
Failures are the pillars of success.

For an aim which is morally sound,
The end and its means justly bound,
Belief in success, hits a summit:
The sky being its only limit!

54

Poetry

Poetry is neither taught nor learned,
It's neither a habit nor addiction,
But just a heart outward turned,
Giving the poet's inner conviction.

Poems can have lots of ceilings–
Rhymes, rhythm and such notions;
But the essence lies in feelings
From the poet's own emotions:

Poems are a cry of passion–
Instinctive calls of grief and delight,
Reflecting the poet's deep commotion,
Drawing attention to its plight.

A poem is wholly subjective–
An outburst from a heated vein;
Such outpourings can't be objective,
Often painting the poet insane.

Poets are *never* in the present–
Seeing things in visionary light,
Often lifting the poem's content
To an abstract figurative height:

They see sparks in mundane things,
Give its reader a pair of wings
To fly to worlds where arts unfold
And move the present to realms untold.

Printed in Great Britain
by Amazon

45577345R00081